Published by McNaughty Books, an imprint of John Napir Ltd

P.O. Box 3353. London N.1. 1SR.

ISBN 1 898505 01 2

Printed and bound in the U.K.

Design by Niamh Lehane.

McNaughty Books

THE McNAUGHTY BOOK
OF
LIMERICKS

Written & Compiled by **Farquhar McNaughty**
Illustrations by **Gray Jolliffe**

CONTENTS

CONTENTS CONTINUED

There once was a Scot called McNaughty

Who, despite being the wrong side of forty,

In his kilt and his vest,

Pursued ladies with zest,

And succeeded more times than he oughtie!.

INTRODUCTION

The limerick packs laughs anatomical

Into space that is quite economical

But the good ones I've seen

So seldom are clean

And the clean ones so seldom are comical.

The limerick can be traced back in various forms to at least the fourteenth century, and was almost invariably associated with bawdy or satirical verse. In particular it was the form often used by wandering beggars singing for their suppers in the sixteenth and seventeenth centuries. Some of these early limericks were published, but most were simply handed down as Folk songs.

However, with the cleansing of published English Language, which started under the general campaigns of moral repression around 1740, the limerick took on its more recent, and not very funny, clean form. In 1820 "The History Of Sixteen Wonderful Old Women" was published, followed in 1822 by "Anecdotes and Adventures of Fifteen Gentlemen" which included the following limerick, generally agreed to have inspired Edward Lear :-

There was a sick man of Tobago

Lived long on rice-gruel and sago

But at last to his bliss

The physician said this -

"To a roast leg of mutton you may go"

In fact there is some doubt as to whether Lear was the sole author of the "Book of Nonsense" which he published in 1846 In any event it was not until after the Book of Nonsense was republished in 1863 and the satirical magazine Punch took up the form, that the limerick really took off.

As a fad the clean limerick lasted some sixty years, with newspapers and magazines offering enormous prizes for supplying the last line. (£3 per week for life was an incredible sum in 1907).

Soon after Lear's book was republished, an imitation called "The New Book of Nonsense" was issued in Philadelphia with profits going to medical relief in the Civil War, a kind of Civil War Comic Relief. This launched the limerick in the USA.

However almost as soon as the clean fad started the bawdy alternatives began circulating in the U.K. written notably by George Sala, Capt Edward Sellon, and the poet Algernon Charles Swinburne. Compare the Edward Lear "Original".

There was an old man of Cape Horn

Who wished he had never been born,

   So he sat on a chair

   'Til he died of despair

That dolorious man of Cape Horn.

with the naughty version possibly by Swinburne:-

There was a young man of Cape Horn

Who wished he had never been born,

    Nor would he have been

    If his father had seen

That the end of the rubber was torn.

In 1870 the first modern collection of naughty limericks was published in London under the title "Cythera's Hymnal or Flakes from the Foreskin". Cythera's Hymnal and limericks published in the erotic magazine The Pearl (London 1879-1880) together with three American collections Immortalia (1927) Some Limericks (1928) and That Immoral Garland (1941) form the basis of all naughty collections published since.

The important point about all these works is that they are collections of limericks which had been passed down over the years by word of mouth. Indeed much of the passing down probably took place in male company with alcoholic assistance, so women were usually the villains or victims, but not always. The following would not be out of place in any feminist alternative humour routine:-

There was a young fellow named Goody

Who claimed that he wouldn't. But would he

If he found himself nude

With a girl in the mood

The question's not would he, but could he ?

Finally comes the question : why is a limerick so-called ? Some say the name comes from a group of Irish poets in Limerick who were writing in this verse form in the middle of the eighteenth century. Some say that a now-forgotten chorus would be sung between each limerick, starting with the words "Won't you come up to Limerick ?" Nobody really knows.

In putting together the "McNaughty Book of Limericks" I have attempted to include those which are both naughty and funny. As humour depends so much on the individual, I'm afraid I will have disapointed those who roar with laughter at coprophilia, venereal diseases or the gratuitous use of four letter words. No doubt they will get their enjoyment elsewhere.

Farquhar McNaughty 1994

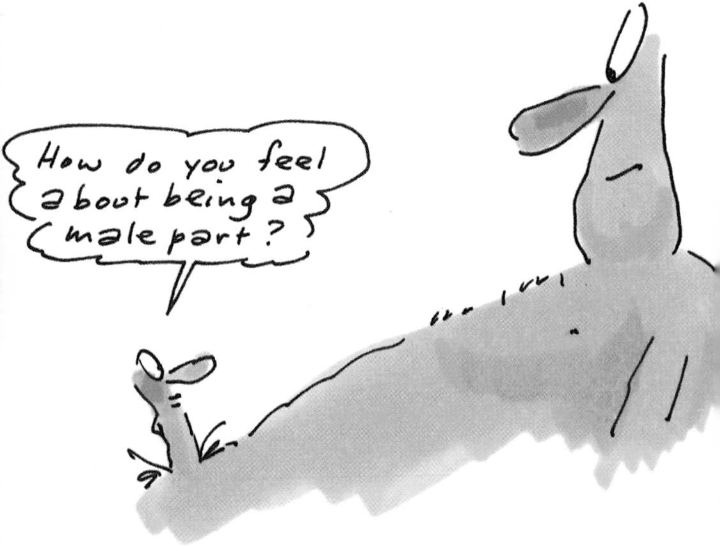
How do you feel about being a male part?

MALE
PARTS

In the garden of Eden lay Adam,

Complacently stroking his madam,

   And loud was his mirth,

   For on all of the earth,

There were only two balls and he had 'em.

✳

There was a young fellow called Lancelot,

Whom his neighbours all looked on askance a lot;

    Whenever he'd pass

    A presentable lass,

The front of his pants would advance a lot.

*

" It's true," confessed Jane, Lady Torres

" That often I beg lifts in lorries,

    When men stop to piss,

    I see things that I miss

When travelling alone in my Morris."

*

"I'll admit," said a lady named Starr,

"That a phallus is like a cigar;

 But to most common people

 A phallic church-steeple

Is stretching the matter too far."

    ✳

There was a young man from Montrose,

Who could tickle himself with his toes.

 He did it so neat

 He fell in love with his feet

And christened them Myrtle and Rose.

    ✳

Said the newly-weds staying near Kitely

"We turn out the electric light nightly.

    Its best to embark

    Upon sex in the dark.

The look of the thing's so unsightly."

✹

There was a young lady of Exeter,

So pretty that men craned their necks at her.

    One was so brave

    As to take out and wave

The distinguishing mark of his sex at her.

✹

There was a young fellow of Kent,

Whose dong was so long that it bent.

    So to save himself trouble

    He put it in double

And instead of coming he went.

✽

There was a young man of Madras

Whose balls were constructed of brass.

    When jangled together

    They played "Stormy Weather"

And lightning shot out of his ass.

✽

When the judge with his wife having sport

Proved suddenly two inches short,

    The good lady declined

    And the judge had her fined

By proving contempt of his court.

There was a young fellow named Bliss

Whose sex life was strangely amiss,

    For even with Venus

    His recalcitrant penis

Would never do better than t
                        h
                        i
                        s

male parts

FEMALE
PARTS

To his bride said the keen eyed detective

"Can it be that my eyesight's defective ?

Has the east tit, the least bit

The best of the west tit,

Or perhaps it's the faulty perspective."

As the elevator car left our floor,

Big Sue caught her tits in the door.

   She yelled a good deal

   But had they been real

She'd have yelled considerably more.

❂

There was a young lady of Bude

Who walked down the street in the nude.

   A bobby said " Whattum

   Magnificent bottom !"

And slapped it as hard as he could.

❂

While I with my usual enthusiasm

Was exploring in Ermentrude's busiasm,

    She explained "They are flat,

    But think nothing of that -

You will find that my sweet sister Susiasm."

          ❋

A vigorous fellow named Bert

Was attracted by every new skirt.

    Oh, it wasn't their minds

    But their rounded behinds

That excited this lovable flirt.

          ❋

There was a young girl of Dumphries

Who said to her man "If you please,

   It would give me great bliss

   Before playing with this.

If you'd pay some attention to these!"

❋

I've a question to ask you, Dear Guest

"Is all that development breast,

   Or can that enormity

   Be a deformity,

Or a poodle perhaps on your chest ?"

❋

NOT
BONKING

Married knock-kneed Edwardo McGuzzum,

Samantha, his bow-legged cousin

  Now some people say

  That love finds a way

But for Ed and Samantha it doesn'.

A bobby of Nottingham Junction

Whose organ had long ceased to function,

    Deceived his good wife

    For the rest of her life

With the aid of his constable's truncheon.

❋

There was an old maid of Duluth

Who wept when she thought of her youth,

    And the glorious chances

    She'd missed at school dances

And once in a telephone booth.

❋

A mortician who practiced in Fife

Made love to the corpse of his wife

   "How could I know, Judge ?

   She was cold, didn't budge

Just the same as she acted in life."

               ❋

A gay guy who lived in Khartoum

Took a lesbian up to his room,

   And they argued all night

   Over who had the right

To do what, and with which, and to whom.

               ❋

Ethnologists up with the Sioux.

Wired home for two punts, one canoe.

   The answer next day

   Said "Girls on the way,

But tell, what the hell's a panoe ?"

✻

"For the tenth time, dull David" said Chloe,

"You have told me my bosom is snowy

   You've made much fine verse on

   Each part of my person

Now <u>do</u> something - there's a good boy!"

✻

A young man by a girl was desired

To give her the thrills she required

    But he died of old age,

    Ere his parts could assuage

The volcanic desire they inspired.

＊

There was a young man of Ostend

Who let a girl play with his end.

    She took hold of Rover

    And felt it all over

And it did what she didn't intend.

＊

There was a young fellow named Goody

Who claimed that he wouldn't. But would he

   If he found himself nude

   With a girl in the mood?

The question's not would he, but could he?

＊

A lisping young lady called Beth

Was saved from a fate worse than death

   Seven times in a row,

   Which unsettled her so

That she quit saying "No" and said "Yeth".

＊

I hope you used a washer that didn't leak
Don't worry–I've been turned off at the mains
LEIGH BOILERS

BONKING

There was a young plumber of Leigh

Who was plumbing a girl by the sea.

She said "Stop your plumbing

There's somebody coming."

Said the plumber, still plumbing, "It's me."

✳

There was a young girl from Hoboken,

Who claimed that her hymen was broken

   From riding a bike

   On a cobblestone pike.

But it really was broken from pokin'.

✷

There was a young lass of Pitlochry

Whose morals seemed rather a mockery

   When they found 'neath her bed,

   A lover, instead

Of the usual item of crockery.

✷

There was a young lady of Gloucester

Whose friends, they all thought they had lost her

   'Til they found on the grass

   The marks of her arse,

And the knees of the man who had crossed her.

Connoisseurs of coition aver

That young British ladies don't stir.

   This condition in Persia

   Is known as inertia,

And is not a response I prefer.

An innocent bride from the mission

Remarked on her first night's coition

   "What an intimate section

   To use for connection.

And, Oh Lord, what a silly position !"

There was a young lady of Joppa

Who became a society cropper.

   She went to Ostend

   With a gentleman friend

And the rest of the story's improper.

There was a young man from the coast

Who had an affair with a ghost.

    At the height of orgasm

    Said the wan ectoplasm

"I think I can feel it - almost !"

✳

A plumber whose name was Ten Brink.

Plumbed the cook as she bent o'er the sink.

    Her resistance was stout

    And Ten Brink petered out

With his pipe-wrench all limber and pink.

✳

"Well I took your advice, Doc" said Knopp

"Told my wife that she'd like it on top.

　　She bounced for an hour,

　　'Til she ran out of power

And the kids, who got bored, made her stop."

※

There was a young lady of Norway

Who hung by her toes in a doorway.

　　She said to her beau

　　"Come over here, Joe,

I think I've discovered one more way!"

※

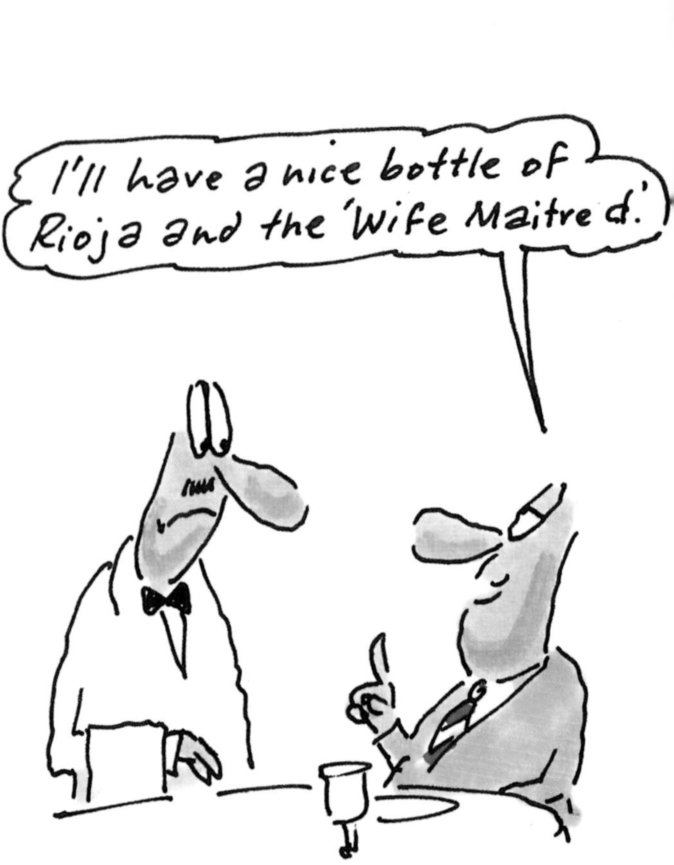
I'll have a nice bottle of Rioja and the 'Wife Maitre d.'

BONKING
LOTS

There once was a sad Maitre d'Hotel

Who said "They can all go to hell

What they do to my wife-

Why, it ruins my life,

And the worst is, they all do it well".

bonking lots

A young lady who taught at Devizes

Was had up at the local assizes,

> For teaching young boys

> Matrimonial joys

And giving French letters as prizes.

✳

There was a young man from Racine

Who invented a bonking machine

> Concave or convex

> It would fit either sex

With attachments for those in-between.

✳

How do you plead?
I dont have to - the little devils can't get enough!

There was a young man with a fiddle

Who questioned his girl "Do you diddle ?"

　　She replied "Yes I do

　　But prefer it with two.

It's twice as much fun in the middle."

＊

Of my husband, I do not ask much

Just an all mod and con little hutch,

　　Bank account in my name,

　　With a cheque book to same,

Plus a small fee for bonking and such.

＊

A famous theatrical actress

Played best in the role of malefactress.

   Yet her home life was pure

   Except, to be sure,

A scandal or two just for practice.

※

A widow whose singular vice

Was to keep her late husband on ice

   Said "It's hard since I lost him,

   I'll never defrost him!

Cold comfort, but cheap at the price."

※

bonking lots

There was a young lady of Bicester

Who was nicer by far than her sister.

    Her sister would giggle

    And wriggle and jiggle

But this one would come if you kissed her.

※

Winter is here with his grouch,

The time when you sneeze and you slouch.

    You can't take your women

    Canoeing or swimmin',

But a lot can be done on the couch.

※

Said Miss Farrow, on one of her larks:

"Sex is more fun in bed than in parks.

    You feel much more at ease

    And your ass doesn't freeze

And passers-by don't make remarks."

※

A wanton young lady of Wimley

Reproached for not acting more primly,

    Answered "Heavens above!

    I know sex isn't love,

But it's such an attractive facsimile."

※

They say as you get older, things get harder – and they're right, thank God!

BONKING
LOTS AND LOTS

The enjoyment of sex, although great,

Is in later years said to abate.

This may well be so,

But how would I know ?

I'm now only seventy-eight.

※

There was a young student called Jones,

Who'd reduce any maiden to moans,

By his wonderful knowledge

Acquired in a college

Of nineteen erogenous zones.

On Saturn the sexes are three.

A nuisance, I think you'll agree.

For performing con brio,

You must have a trio,

While it even takes two for a pee.

bonking lots and lots

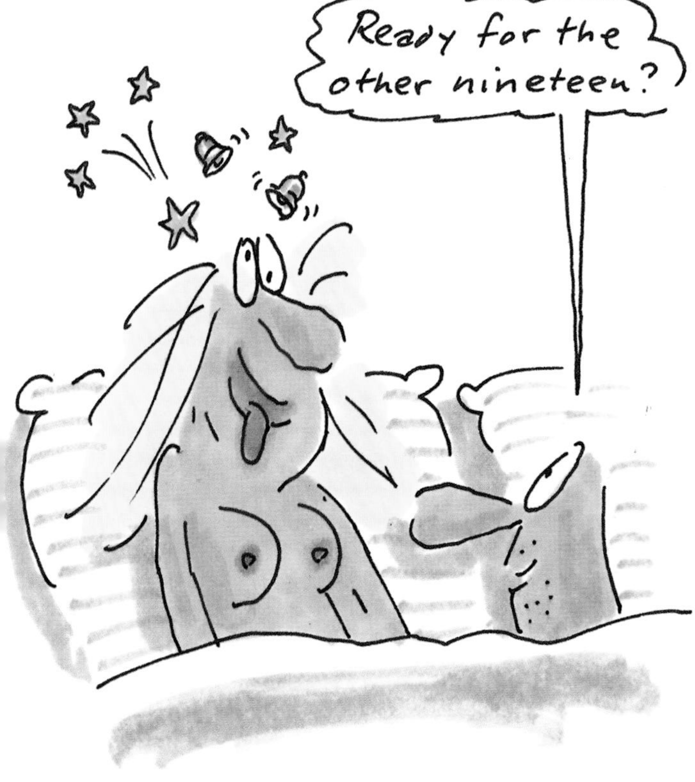
Ready for the other nineteen?

There was a young lady of Trent,

Who said that she knew what it meant

When men asked her to dine

With cocktails and wine,

She knew what it meant - but she went.

✳

There was a young woman in Dee

Who stayed with each man she did see.

If it came to a test

She wished to be best

And practice makes perfect you see.

✳

There was a young lady called Flynn

Who thought fornication a sin,

    But when she was tight

    It seemed quite all right

So everyone filled her with gin.

❇

There was a young lady called Smith

Whose virtue was mainly a myth.

    She said "Try as I can

    I can't find a man

That it's fun to be virtuous with."

❇

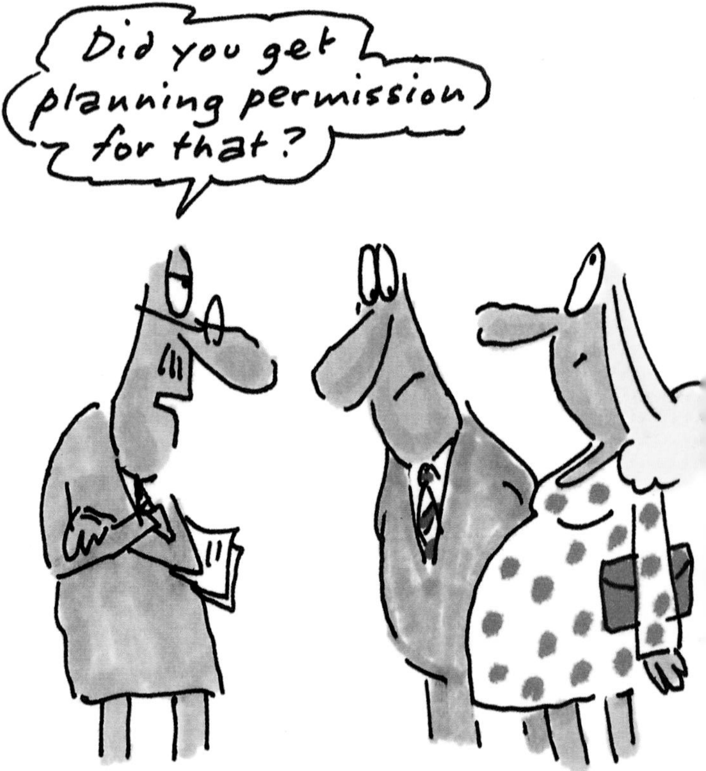
Did you get planning permission for that?

NINE MONTHS LATER

There was a young lady of Wantage.

Of whom the Town Clerk took advantage.

   Said the County Surveyor

   "Of course you must pay her,

You've altered the line of her frontage."

I once met a girl on a train

Who declared she'd a man on the brain.

   But to judge from her size

   And the look in her eyes.

It wasn't her brain he'd been layin'.

＊

There was a young girl who begat

Three brats, by name Nat, Pat and Tat.

   It was fun in the breeding,

   But hell in the feeding

When she found there was no tit for tat.

＊

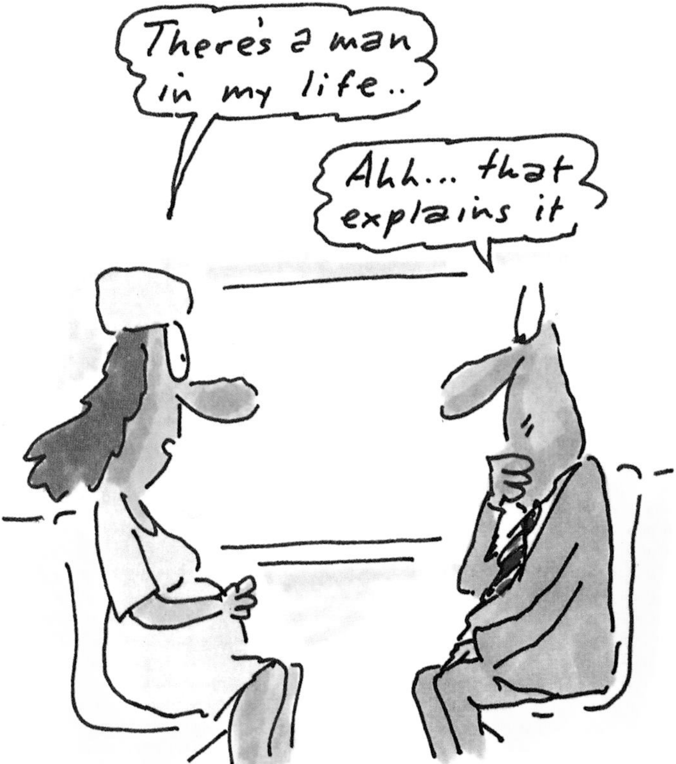
There's a man in my life..
Ahh... that explains it

There was a young lady of Louth

Who suddenly grew very stout.

   Her mother said "Nelly,

   There's more in your belly

Than ever went in through your mouth."

There was a young girl from Penzance

Who decided to take just one chance.

   So she let herself go

   In the arms of her beau,

And now all her sisters are aunts.

There was a young man of Cape Horn

Who wished he had never been born.

   Nor would he have been

   If his father had seen

That the tip of the condom was torn.

❋

There was a young lady called Wylde,

Who kept herself quite undefiled

   By thinking of Jesus,

   Contagious diseases,

And the bother of having a child.

❋

KNICKERS ETC'

There was a young lady called Etta,

Who fancied herself in a sweater

  Three reasons she had:

  "Keeping warm" wasn't bad,

But the other two reasons were better.

✳

There was a young woman from Aenos

Who came to our party as Venus.

   We told her how rude

   'Twas to come there quite nude,

And we brought her a leaf from the greenhouse.

✳

There was a young girl from Darjeeling

Who could dance with such exquisite feeling

   There was never a sound

   For miles around

Save of fly-buttons hitting the ceiling.

✳

Her ladyship wonders if you'd care to wear this or you may catch cold

Try our rubber girlfriend (air - inflatable)

Perennially young (quite insatiable).

   Say our satisfied clients

   From mere midgets to giants:

"She's incredibly sexy and mateable."

⁕

There was a young monk of Kilkyre

Who was smitten with carnal desire.

   The immediate cause

   Was the abbess' drawers,

Which were hung up to dry by the fire.

⁕

A sailor who slept in the sun

Woke to find his fly-buttons undone.

 He remarked with a smile,

 "Jesus Christ, a sundial!

And now it's a quarter past one!"

    *

A reformer who went out to Bali

To change the sartorial folly

 Of the girls, now admits

 "A pair of good tits,

In season, can seem rather jolly."

There once was a harlot at Hayle

With her price-list tattooed on her tail,

    And on her behind,

    For the sake of the blind,

She had it embroidered in Braille.

※

There was a young lady of Erskine

And the chief of her charms was her fairskin

    But the sable she wore

    (She had several more)

She had earned it whilst wearing her bareskin.

※

There was a young woman from Wilts

Who went up to Scotland on stilts.

   When they said "Oh how shocking

   To show so much stocking!"

She answered "Well, how about kilts?"

✳

A bottle of perfume that Willie sent

Was highly displeasing to Millicent.

   Her thanks were so cold,

   That they quarrelled, I'm told

'Cos Willie sent Millicent silly scent.

✳

CLERICAL
ERRORS

A minister up in Vermont

Keeps goldfish alive in his font.

  When he dips the babes in,

  They tickle the skin,

Which is all that the innocents want.

There was a young lady of Chichester

Whose tits made the saints in their niches stir.

One morning at matins

In very tight satins

She made the Bishop of Chichester's britches stir.

✳

From the crypt of the church of St Giles,

Came a cry that resounded for miles.

Said the vicar " Good Gracious!

Has Father Ignatius

Forgotten the Bishop has piles."

✳

clerical errors

A handsome young monk in a wood

Told a girl she should cling to the good

   She obeyed him, but gladly,

   He repulsed her, but sadly,

And said she had misunderstood.

✲

There was a young monk from Siberia

Whose morals were very inferior.

   He did to a nun

   What he shouldn't have done

And now she's a mother superior.

✲

When Paul the Apostle lay prostrate

And leisurely prodded his prostate

 With pride parabolic

 His most apostolic

Appendage became an apostate.

*

There was a young laundress of Lamas

Who invented high amorous dramas

 For the spots she espied

 Dried and hardened inside

The pants of the parson's pyjamas.

*

I once had the wife of a Dean

Seven times while the Dean was out ski-in.

   She remarked with some gaiety

   "Not bad for the laity

But the Bishop once managed thirteen."

                   ✳

There was a young lady called Alice

Who peed in a catholic chalice.

   She said "I did this

   From a great need to piss

And not from sectarian malice."

                   ✳

There once was a girl from Cape Cod

Who dreamt she'd been buggered by God.

   But 'tweren't the Almighty

   That lifted her nighty,

But Roger, the lodger, the sod.

✷

Astute Melanesians on Munda,

Heard a parson discussing the wunda

   Of virginal birth

   They debated its worth,

Then tore the poor padre asunda.

✷

NAUGHTY
KNOWLEDGE

As Titian was mixing rose-madder

His model reclined on a ladder.

Her position to Titian

Suggested coition,

So he leapt up the ladder and had'er.

A publisher went off to France

In search of a tale of romance.

A Parisian lady

Told a story so shady

That the publisher made an advance.

※

Said the Duchess of Alba to Goya

"Paint some pictures to hang in my foyer!"

So he painted her twice

In the nude, to look nice,

And then once in her clothes, to annoya.

※

A mathematician named Hall

Had an almost rectangular ball,

    And the cube of its weight

    Times his pecker, plus eight

Was four fifths, of five eighths, of sod all.

           ※

There was a young artist called Saint,

Who swallowed some samples of paint.

    All the shades of the spectrum

    Flowed out of his rectum

With colourful lack of restraint.

           ※

Said Einstein "I have an equation,

Which science might call Rabelasian,

   Let P be virginity

   Approaching infinity

And U be a constant : persuasion.

"Now if P over U be inverted,

And the square root of U be inserted.

   X times over P

   The result, Q.E.D.

Is a relative," Einstein asserted.

※

In the speech of his time, did the Bard

Refer to his dong as his "Yard,"

But sigh no more, madams

'Twas no longer than Adam's

Or mine, and not one half so hard.

※

A young schizophrenic named Struther

When told of the death of his brother

Said "Yes, it's too bad

But I can't feel too sad -

After all, I still have each other."

※

There was an old sculptor named Phidias

Whose knowledge of Art was invidious.

    He carved Aphrodite

    Without any nightie

Which startled the purely fastidious.

＊

An old archaeologist, Throstle,

Discovered a marvellous fossil.

    He knew from its bend,

    And the knob on its end,

'Twas the peter of Paul the Apostle.

＊

ANIMAL ATTRACTIONS

There was an old Scot called McTavish

Who attempted an anthropoid ravish.

   But the object of rape

   Was the wrong sex of ape,

And the anthropoid ravished McTavish.

*

There was a young girl from Dundee

Who was raped by an ape in a tree.

    The result was quite horrid,

    All ass and no forehead

Three balls and a purple goatee.

✳

There was a young gaucho named Bruno

Who said "Bonking is one thing I do know,

    A woman is fine,

    And a sheep is divine,

But a llama is Numero Uno."

✳

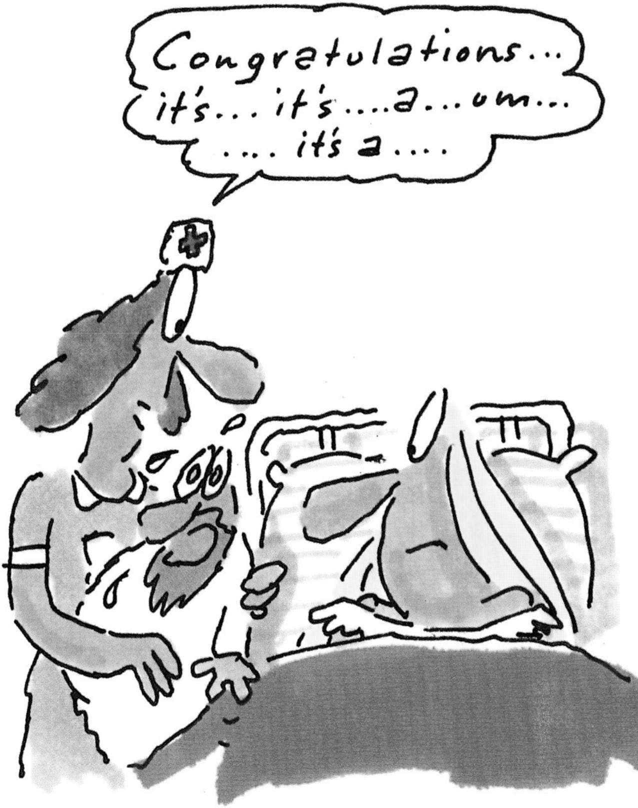
Congratulations... it's... it's....a...um... .... it's a....

There once was a fairy named Cyril

Who was had in a wood by a squirrel.

    And he liked it so good

    That he stayed in the wood

Just as long as the squirrel was virile.

※

There was a young man of St John's

Who wanted to bugger the swans

    But the loyal hall-porter

    Said "Pray take my daughter!

Them birds are reserved by the Dons."

※

There was a young lady named Myrtle

Who had an affair with a turtle.

   Next morning at dawn

   She started to spawn

Which proves that the turtle was fertile.

※

There was a young girl from Peru.

Who'd a dog and a cat and a gnu.

   From a sailor named Harrot,

   She bought an old parrot

And he threw in a young cockatoo.

※

animal attractions

A lady while dining in Crewe

Found an elephant's whang in her stew

Said the waiter, "Don't shout

And don't wave it about

Or the others will all want one too."

※

There was a young peasant called Gorse

Who fell madly in love with his horse.

Said his wife "You rapscallion

That horse is a stallion -

This constitutes grounds for divorce."

※

A habit obscene and bizarre

Has taken a-hold of papa.

He brings home young camels

And other odd mammals,

And leaves them alone with mama.

＊

There was a young fellow called Price

Who dabbled in all sorts of vice.

He had virgins and boys

And mechanical toys,

And on Mondays he meddled with mice.

＊

PHARTING

There was a young girl of La Plata,

Who was widely renowned as a farter.

   Her deafening reports

   At the Argentine sports

Made her much in demand as a starter.

※

There was a young girl from Australia

Who painted her ass as a dahlia.

The drawing was fine,

And the colour divine

But the scent, on the whole, was a failure.

There was a young fellow named Charted

Who rubbed soap on his bum when it smarted,

And to his surprise

He received a grand prize

For the bubbles he blew when he farted.

There was a young man named McBride

Who could fart whenever he tried

    In a contest he blew

    Two thousand and two

And then shat, and was disqualified.

✳

There was a young fellow from Sparta

A truly magnificent farter

    On the strength of one bean

    He'd fart "God Save the Queen"

And Beethoven's Moonlight Sonata.

✳

I sat by the Duchess at tea

And she asked "Do you fart when you pee?"

   I said with some wit

   "Do you belch when you shit?"

And felt it was one up for me.

✳

Sir Reginald Barrington, Bart.

Went to the masked ball as a fart.

   He had painted his face

   Like a more private place,

And his voice made the dowagers start.

✳

CHAUVINIST
PIGGERY

There once was a monarch of Spain

Who was terribly haughty and vain.

   When women were nigh,

   He would open his fly,

And poke them with sneers of disdain.

※

There was a young fellow of Lyme

Who lived with three wives at a time.

When asked "Why the third ?"

He replied "One's absurd,

And bigamy, Sir, is a crime."

＊

A rooster residing in Spain

Used to service his hens in the rain.

"I give them a bloody

Good time when it's muddy,

Which stops them from getting too vain."

＊

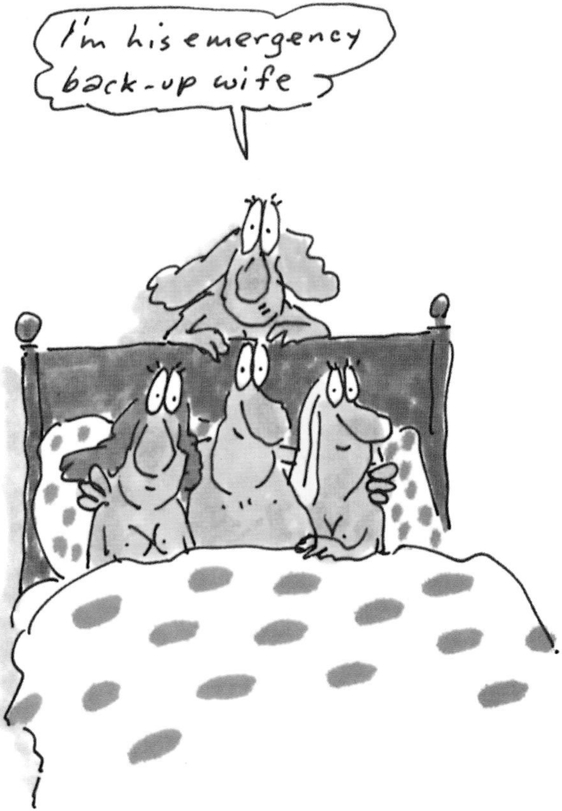
I'm his emergency back-up wife

A self-centred young fellow named Newcombe

Who seduced many girls but made few come,

 Said "The pleasures of tail

 Were ordained for the male.

I've had mine. Do I care whether you come ?"

✳

There was a young fellow called Wyatt

Who had a big girl on the quiet,

 But down on the wharf

 He kept a nice dwarf

Just in case he should go on a diet.

✳

It seems I impregnated Marge,

So I do rather feel by and large

   Some dough should be tendered,

   For services rendered,

But I can't quite decide what to charge.

✳

Though his plan when he gave her a buzz

Was to do what man normally does,

   She declared: " I'm a soul

   Not a sexual goal."

So he shrugged and called someone who was.

✳

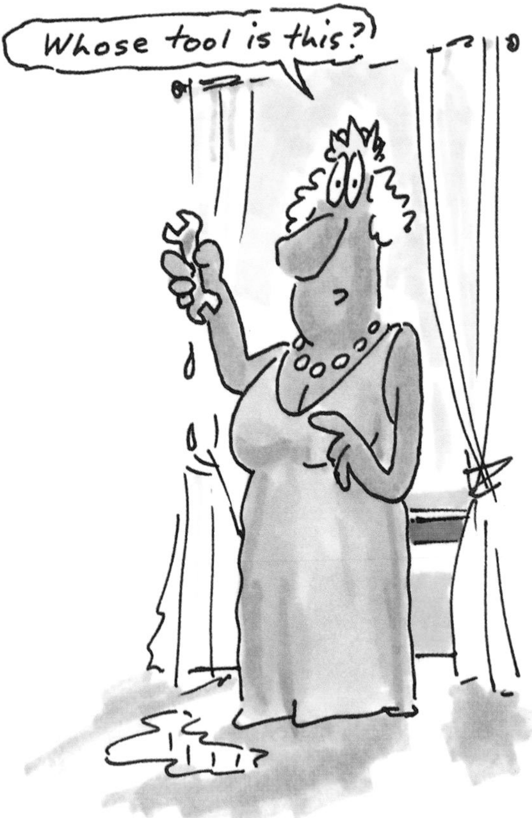
Whose tool is this?

MALE PARTS DETACHED

After lunch the old Duchess of Teck.

Observed "If you'll listen one sec,

   We've found a man's tool

   In the small swimming pool,

So would all of you gentlemen check ?"

*

There was a young sailor called Bates

Who did the fandango on skates.

He fell on his cutlass

Which rendered him nutless

And practically useless on dates.

※

Did you hear about young Henry Lockett ?

He was blown down the street by a rocket.

The force of the blast

Blew his balls up his ass,

And his pecker was found in his pocket.

※

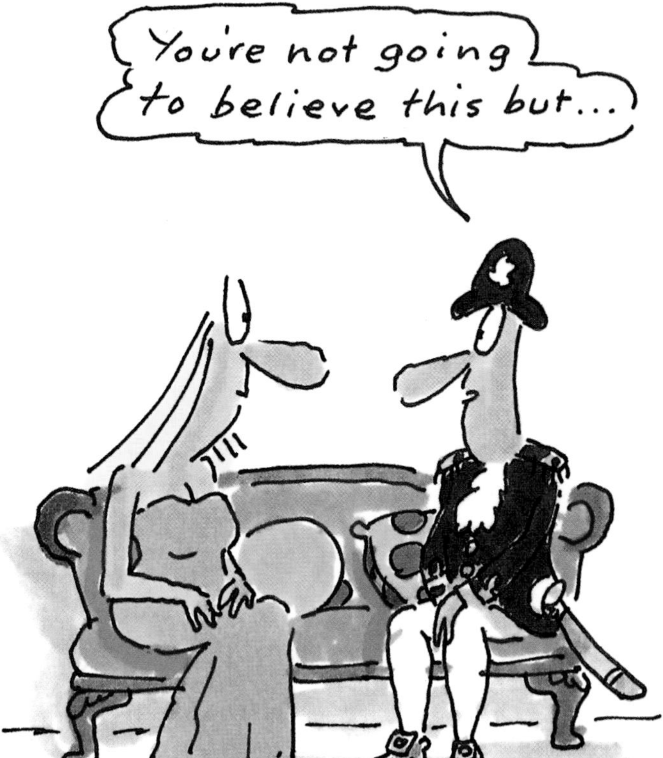
You're not going to believe this but...

There once was a young girl called Rhoda

Who constructed herself a pagoda,

And the walls of the halls

Were festooned with the balls

And the tools of the fools who bestrode her.

✳

There was a young singer named Springer

Got his testicles caught in the wringer.

He hollered in pain

As they rolled down the drain

"There goes my career as a singer."

✳

There once was a young man of Datchet

Who cut off his dong with a hatchet

   Then very politely

   He sent it to Whitley

And ordered a copy to match it.

✳

And then there's the story that's fraught

With disaster - of balls that got caught,

   When a chap took a crap

   In the woods, and a trap

Underneath.... Oh I can't bear the thought!

✳

INDEX

INDEX CONTINUED

ANNUAL LIMERICK COMPETITION

The Annual Limerick Competition offers a first prize of a weekend for two in Limerick, Eire, inclusive of airfares, hotel, meals etc. In addition the author of any Limerick published by McNaughty Books in any future publications will receive £5. The deadline for entries will be 31st March each year. Entries received after that year will go forward for the following year's competition.

COMPETITION RULES FOR
THE ANNUAL LIMERICK COMPETITION

1. The competition in this book is open to anyone aged 18 or over except employees and their families of the publishers, its printers and anyone else connected with the competition.

P.T.O.➡

2. Entries must be set out on the entry coupon.

3. There is no cash alternative to the weekend in Limerick, and transport will be provided to Limerick only from the address on the entry form.

4. No responsibility can be accepted for entries which are delayed, damaged, mislaid or wrongfully delivered.

5. Each entry shall be an original limerick and all entrants agree to the publication of their limerick in any future book by the publishers, and in any associated publicity.
   If an entry is published the entrant will receive £5 upon its initial publication.

6. The decision of the judges will be final and winners will be notified by post. No correspondense can be entered into.

7. Entry implies acceptance of these rules.

8. The closing date is 31st March annually.
   Entries received after that date will go forward for the following year's competition.

Annual Limerick Competition

_____

_____

_____

_____

_____

I have read the rules for the Annual Limerick Competition
and agree to be bound by them. This is my original Limerick.

Signature   Date

PTO →

Name

Address

Town   Zip/Post Code

Country

Post entries to: The Annual Limerick Competition
John Napir Ltd, P.O. Box 3353, London N1-1SR, United Kingdom.

Annual Limerick Competition

_____

_____

_____

_____

_____

I have read the rules for the Annual Limerick Competition
and agree to be bound by them. This is my original Limerick.

Signature   Date   PTO ←

Name

Address

Town   Zip/Post Code

Country

Post entries to: The Annual Limerick Competition
John Napir Ltd, P.O. Box 3353, London N1-1SR, United Kingdom.

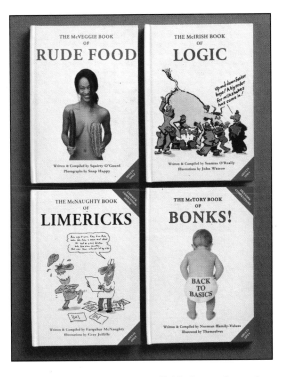

McNaughty Books are available from all good
Book and Gift shops, or direct from the
publishers John Napir Ltd at P O Box 3353,
London N1 - 1SR at £4.99 per copy.